The Young Muslim's Mindful Book of Wellbeing

Muslim Children's Books

With special thanks to
Abu Bakr Brown

Published by Muslim Children's Books
Suite H, 31-33 College Road, Harrow, Middlesex HA1 1EJ

muslimchildrensbooks.co.uk

Published by Muslim Children's Books 2018
© Zanib Mian, 2018

Moral rights asserted.

ISBN 978-0-9955406-7-5

Contents

Read it in order the first time!

How to Be Happy

Real happiness isn't linked to anything, or anyone; only to Allah. It's when you can be happy for no apparent reason, so much so that you beam!

Being happy, all the way, deep into your heart, is a very special feeling. It can only happen when you are at peace with yourself and you are passing your days, doing things that Allah loves and shines down his pleasure on you, for doing . It's as if the happy feelings that you are having are actually Allah's love, shining through all your insides, with no negative thoughts to spoil it.

This is real happiness, which feels better and lasts longer than the happiness you get from things like winning a prize, or getting a new thing.

That kind of happiness just goes away if you lose or break the thing. Some people keep waiting for happiness, because they think they will be happy when they finally get the new toy they wanted, or pass their exams. But you don't have to WAIT for real happiness, you can have it now, because the things you are waiting for are not what are going to make you happy.

Feeling Allah close to you and connecting to Him can make you feel this real happiness. That is all part of having a happy mind and heart, which this book will show you how to do, insha'Allah. You can even grab this happiness at times where you would have thought it's hard to be happy, by turning your thoughts to Allah, talking to Him and feeling Him watching you, with love.

Some of the things that Allah loves, and so make you feel really happy are; talking to Him, or talking about him to others; being good to your family and other people; helping others; doing things that make this world a better place, and of course; praying, and reciting Qur'an. But, also, even when you're doing other 'normal' things like going shopping, or reading a book, or going to school - as long as they are all things that Allah likes, you will still feel peace and happiness. That's because, as Muslims, everything we do makes Allah happy, if we are doing them knowing He's there.

There are some things that you should beware of, because they can get in the way of you being happy. They are happiness destroyers, for example; wanting things you don't have, jealousy, and other negative thoughts. And there are other things, that can help you be happy. This book will take you through all of them.

☀ Negative Thoughts
vs Positive Thoughts

What you think inside your head has a big affect on you. It controls how you feel, but also how other people feel about you.

Being positive means that you are hopeful and confident and that you think of things and people, in a good way rather than a bad way. Being negative is the opposite of that. If you are being negative, you might be telling yourself that you can't do something, or that you're bad at it. And you might think that someone wants to harm you (bad expectations). For Muslims, positive thoughts are also about Allah and knowing He is there with us and loving us.

Our thoughts can completely change the way we behave, and how well we can do things. That's because positive thoughts are like a bright, beautiful light inside you.

Negative thoughts are like darkness. If you think about it, light always shines and gets rid of the darkness. In a dark room, when you turn the light on, there is no more darkness.

And if you don't have any light, the darkness will always be there.

Now imagine you tried to solve a puzzle in the dark, or paint a beautiful picture, or even walk, or jump, or cook, or anything! You might be able to get it done, but it certainly wouldn't be very good, because the darkness would have spoilt it all. You might even end up spilling the paint, or losing the puzzle pieces, or stepping on something, because you couldn't see properly.

Now, if you had a little bit of light, you could have done it better, and if you had lots of light you could have done it perfectly!

13

That's how positive thoughts can help you do things better. You're keeping the light on, instead of doing them in the dark. Having positive thoughts, can make you feel really peaceful, happy and full of bouncy energy, because you have a bright light shining inside you. And with these good thoughts, no matter what you're doing; your schoolwork, projects, or even just talking to people, it will be done excellently!

Having negative thoughts can make you feel grumpy and tired and can stop you from doing things well, because you're doing them with no light.

What's more, other people can feel your thoughts. Even if you never say a word, people can feel whether you are thinking positive things, or negative things. They won't even know that what they feel is because of the thoughts in your head, but they will feel great around you, if you have good thoughts and they will feel quite terrible around you if you have bad thoughts.

Just as they shine inside you, good thoughts shine out of you too! It's as if you can share your light with other people. If you have lots of these positive thoughts, you might be able to make people feel better, just by being near them. You'll see when you get to the 'Shining from Inside' section.

If you have angry, jealous, and negative thoughts, they can make people react to you in a bad way. People suck up the anger inside you and start behaving the same way as you are feeling.

The great news is, that with a good flow of positive thoughts, you will always be cool.

Allah Loves You

We all know how much a mother loves her child. She does everything she can to keep the child safe and happy. She even gives up things she really loves, for him/her. When the child gets hurt, she feels sad. When the child is upset, she makes him/her feel better again. In fact, there is nothing that a mother wouldn't do for her child. That's a lot of love!

But there's something really amazing about Allah and you: Allah loves you seventy times more than a mother loves her child. If your mother's, father's, or the love of anyone who cares for you, feels so good, and so strong, imagine what Allah's love is like. You are constantly being looked after by Allah, with all that love.

If you have a think about this, it really is mind-blowing! The Master of the Entire Universe loves YOU. When the one who controls every single thing that happens, loves YOU with this huge amount of love, how can anything happen to you that isn't fantastic? Even the things that don't seem so fantastic, actually are. They are out of love too, just like when your adult stops you from doing something that you wanted to do, because it wasn't good for you (see 'The Bigger Picture').

You can really feel this sensational love from Allah, if you do things right - and it feels super! Allah shows it in lots of different ways if you trust Him with all your heart, talk to Him all the time, live your life the way He wants, and stay connected to Him through your prayers. Always put Allah first. The best things happen when you do all this.

Say, 'See! Allah loves me,' whenever you feel that something has happened to you because of Allah's love. Soon, you will be saying it all the time, because as you get through this book, you'll realise that Allah's love is all around you and you'll want to shout it from the rooftops!

How to Deal With Worry and Bad Expectations

When something is happening that makes a person feel anxious and worried, often, they let themselves become that worry. They become a whole other person: Captain Worry Pants.

The thing about Captain Worry Pants is that he can't make sure that the things that he is worried about, go smoothly. He can't even think straight because he is too busy worrying and expecting bad things to happen to him.

But when you're expecting something bad to happen to you, it means you're expecting that Allah will *let* bad things happen to you. Allah has said that He will be how we expect Him to be. So if we expect that He won't let anything bad happen, that He will take care of us, then He will! Also, Captain Worry Pants is controlled by negative thoughts. We all know now, why those are bad.

How to keep worry away:

Talk to Allah about the things that are making you worry. Ask Him to take care of them. It's the greatest feeling ever, to leave things to Allah, when you know that He's by your side, loving and protecting you. If you talk to Him and trust in Him completely, He will not let you down.

Keep shining, and have good expectations of Allah, yourself and others.

Go and face the things you're worrying about, with a smile and trust in Allah. Do your best, with all your happy and positive energy. Don't **be** the worry.
Be **you!**

And remember, that trusting Allah means that you will be happy with whatever happens after that, because you know that Allah knows what's best for you. Sometimes, even if we stop worrying, things still might not go the way we hoped, but that's OK too. To find out why, see 'The Bigger Picture', and 'How to Feel OK If You Wanted Something, but Didn't Get It'.

There's A Way Out of Every Problem ...

YOU can find it. Especially with
these tips...

1. Ask Allah, and be
sure that He will help
you.

2. Smile

Asking Allah

When you ask Allah, you're asking the one with all the power, to help you. What better help could you get!? It's like when you ask an adult to help you with something tricky and you feel sure that they'll be able to do it, because they're an adult. Asking Allah for help is even better! As long as you are sure that Allah is listening and He will help you - He will! This doesn't mean that you can't ask someone else for help, if you need it. But you just have to ask Allah first. That way, however you solve the problem, whether it's by yourself, or with someone else, you know it's Allah's way of helping you.

Smiling

Yes! Everything is better with a smile. When you smile, you feel positive and strong, so you can think about the problem clearly, and without becoming Captain Worry Pants! Also, your brain works better and you look good too!

☀ The Bigger Picture

When something upsetting happens to us, it can be very hard. But, just like one piece of a huge puzzle, which might look ugly on its own, that upsetting thing makes up part of a bigger, beautiful picture when all the pieces come together.

When bad things happen, we might even start wondering how Allah can let them happen to us, especially if He loves us. What you have to remember is that He DOES love you, and He knows better, even if you don't understand it yet. Everything that happens to you, whether you see it as a good thing or a bad thing, is because Allah loves you.

Even if it's a bit topsy-turvy, you're getting somewhere great in the end!

Sometimes things happen to us which make us feel fed up, but then years later, we realise that if it hadn't happened, then we wouldn't be in this great place in our lives, right now. So even though it was hard at the time, it was part of the bigger picture, which only Allah can see. Only He knows the full plan of your life, and why some things need to happen to be able to make other great things happen.

If you looked at a room, through the keyhole in the door, you would only be able to see a tiny bit of what is going on inside it. Our lives are like that, we can only see what's happening right now, we can't see how it fits with what will happen in the future. What we see through the keyhole might be scary and confusing, but if we could see everything else in the room, it would make sense and be ok.

So, if something happens that you don't like, be brave with your heart. Allah is holding it, and you are right where you're supposed to be. He knows what He is doing and it will work out best for you and everyone else. This trust in Allah and His plan is a fantastic feeling. When you can feel it, even if you were on a rocket shooting into the sky, you would know that Allah is taking you somewhere, and He will always catch you.

 # Friends

The way you feel inside, depends a fair bit on the people you spend lots of time with. That's why it's important to know how to choose good friends.

A friend is...

A smile in your heart. Someone who sees you and likes you, just the way you are. When you see them, a real smile spreads across your face, like a warm marshmallow wave. A friend is someone whose words never bite or sting. Someone who makes you feel good, even if they have to point out a mistake you made. If you have a friend, even one, thank Allah for them. They are precious.

How to Feel OK If You Wanted Something, but Didn't Get It...

Sometimes, when people want something, they can't stop thinking about it and carry the 'wanting' around with them like a huge, heavy weight. Even though they can't do anything about it. And if they don't get it, the 'wanting' gets even bigger, and heavier, and then they carry that around too.

But, you don't have to carry your 'wanting'. You can just pass it to Allah T'aala to carry for you. Because He's the only one that can give you that thing, anyway. That way, you can try for the thing you want, without the worrying.

And not worry about the thing, if you didn't get it.

It's pointless wanting something Allah thought best not to give you anyway.

Jealousy and Being Happy With What You Have

Sometimes, people see something that someone else has and they wish that they had it. They wish this so much that they feel angry that the other person has it, and sometimes they're even mean to that person for having it.

If you remember that Allah is in control of your life and the things you have in it, it's easy to feel happy with what you have, or don't have. Only Allah can decide who has what. If you don't have it, Allah thought it best that you don't!

This also means that the things that you do have, are from Allah. Whether you think they are fantastic or not, they are yours. They were chosen for you by the Lord of the Worlds! They are gifts from Allah, who can take them away, or give you more any time He wants.

Allah loves people who feel happy with the things they have. This is called gratefulness. Allah likes to give grateful people more.

So, enjoy what you have, make the most of it and thank Allah for it.

# Feeling Sad

It's ok to feel sad. You are allowed to be sad and to feel the sadness. The only thing is, you shouldn't hold onto it and keep it forever. Once you've thought about why you are sad, and what you will do to make things better, you can turn your sadness into something else, like this little girl does...

When I feel sad,

I close my eyes. I smile.
It's not a real smile. Not in the
beginning. But then,
my brain starts to wonder why my
face is smiling. And it remembers lots
of reasons. Lots and lots!
You are there, Allah, watching me. That makes my smile bigger.
And real. And it stays there on my face, all day long.

☀ Talking to Allah

Nothing feels more comforting and joyful than having a 'heart to heart' with Allah.

We all need lots of love and hugs from our loved ones, when something is going on that is hard to handle. That's great and you should do that, but also, you should talk to Allah.

It makes perfect sense to talk to Allah all the time, about everything, especially our problems, because Allah is the only one who has power and control over them. You can tell Him all about what's bothering you and ask Him to take care of it. Then you still have to do what you can as a human being on this Earth, but remember that you handed the problem over to the Master of the Universe, so get on with things happily - you're in great hands!

What's really exciting, is that as soon as we start speaking to Allah, He is there, listening, with so much love! You don't need any special devices to speak to Allah, like you do to speak to people. You don't even have to do it out loud - you can say things to Him in your heart - and when you do it, when you start talking to Him, knowing He's there and how much He loves you and how much He can help - it feels fantastic! He loves it when we depend on Him and ask Him for help, or tell Him how worried we are, or how happy we are.

We don't only have to talk to Allah when something huge comes up. He's there for the little things too, even the tiny little things. Also, we can do it in any language and any place. And the best thing is that when we talk to Allah, we can be ourselves completely, because He already knows everything about us. We have no secrets from Allah, so we don't need to pretend about anything. He's the one that knows you and is there for you exactly as you are.

Get used to always asking Him first, whenever you need something, and telling Him how happy you are when something great is happening to you.

Every day, find a quiet place where you can be alone. Sit and let yourself be calm. Think about Allah and that He is there, listening to you. Talk to Him about anything you want. You don't even have to speak out loud. Enjoy the moment - it's just Allah and you. Soon, you'll be able to 'go into your heart,' even in a noisy place, to talk to Allah; your closest friend.

Getting Closer to Allah ☀ Through Nature

Have you ever looked at the sky, or a tree, or a mountain and felt closer to Allah?

Sometimes, we can know a bit more about a person, or even feel close to them if they write us a nice letter, or show us something that they made. Nature is full of things that Allah has made, and they can really help us to feel Him close.

We look at the sky and the trees all the time. Because they are around us, our eyes just happen to fall on them. But we don't always **see** them. Seeing is different to looking, because to see, you use your mind and your heart. You use all of you. All of your attention. You go deeper than just looking. And when you do that, you can feel yourself becoming peaceful and happy inside, because you are looking at something that is perfect and beautiful. Something that is proof of Allah's magnificence and of how perfect He is!

Allah wants us to be able to **see** nature and be reminded of Him. He knows that if we know He is there, we will think of Him and feel close to Him by looking at the beautiful things He has created.

You can use nature to feel closer to Allah. Just try this:

Look at some magnificent part of nature; a tree, the sky, the ocean, a mountain, a flower, or anything else. Choose one to focus on. But don't just look at it. **Be there** with it. Marvel at it. Watch it: how it behaves, how it moves (if it moves), and how it makes you feel ...

Let yourself wonder and stare. Don't think about anything else. Don't look at anything else. Keep breathing smoothly. Do this until you feel something different inside you – until you feel something wonderful inside you. That's every part of you realising that Allah is there and He is absolutely amazing, for creating such a thing. Soon, you will **feel** Allah there too, and it will be awesome. You can say subhaan'Allah with your tongue, or just in your heart.

What if it's not happening?

If it's not happening, you can go through this book and make sure you have followed all the other bits first. If you haven't been able to get rid of negative thoughts and jealousy and wanting things, then this part will be tricky to do.

Also, make sure you've stopped thinking about everything else. If you're thinking about how much homework you have waiting for you, or that you can't wait to hop onto the games console again, this won't work.

Now you can do this any time you want. Even if there's barely any nature around you, you can just look up at the sky and feel closer to Allah.

Being Around Negative People

Sometimes, you might come across people who have lots of negative thoughts inside them. You might be able to see this, because they aren't shining and they might be behaving in ways that their bad thoughts are making them behave. Remember, people can have negative thoughts because of jealousy, bad expectations, or wanting things. Not everyone has learnt how to have good thoughts, like you have.

The good news is that even though other people's negative thoughts can make **you** feel down too, you can control it. You can do this by making sure your thoughts stay postive and good! Even if someone is saying or doing something that you don't like, don't let yourself be sucked in. In fact, you have to make sure you shine even brighter, so your light will be more powerful than their negativity.

Maybe you can even help them - not by telling them how they should think and behave, but by talking about something peaceful and happy, like Allah! What will happen, is that they will come away feeling less negative than before.

Once in a while, someone will say something to you that will hurt your heart because it feels unfair. To help yourself feel ok after something like that, you can remind yourself that there is probably something troubling that person. If they were happy, peaceful, close to Allah, and shining, like you, they wouldn't feel the need to say horrible things to others.

You can make dua that Allah makes them feel better and you can also talk to Allah about how you feel. Ask yourself: *how can that person's words hurt me?* Just because they said it, it doesn't mean it's true, or that they can make anything happen to you. Only Allah can do that. Also, perhaps look at the 'When I Feel Sad' section.

And most importantly, carry on being a real star!

☀ Shining From Inside

Everything in this book, will make you shine from the inside, if you do it properly.

When you shine, people will wonder what it is you have, that they don't! They will look at you and wonder what makes you shine so much that they feel happy just being next to you – even if they didn't feel so good before!

That's the wonderful thing about shining from the inside, it makes **you** feel good and others feel good too! Just imagine, that people have shields that reflect back whatever you are giving. So if you are shining out love and peace, people will shine it back at you, without even knowing why! If you are bursting with anger and bad feelings, people will reflect that right back at you, and feel like being horrid to you.

How to shine

When you start doing everything you have learnt through this book, you will automatically start shining. It can all be summed up with the two things below:

1. Being connected to Allah

You know that you are being looked after by Allah, who loves you even more than your mum, so He won't let anything happen to you that's not absolutely fabulous for you. When you know that Allah loves you, you are close to Him. You talk to Him more and think about Him more, and you trust Him. When you look at nature, it reminds you of Allah and His greatness.

Because of all this, you are connected to Allah. You know He's there, all the time. You feel great!

2. Good, happy thoughts about people and your life. You have happy, positive thoughts. You're not waiting for something to happen to make you happy because you have real happiness, now. You're not carrying your 'wanting' around. And you're not waiting for bad things to happen. You're not jealous of anyone and you're not afraid, because you trust in Allah. When sad things happen, you know how to let go of the sadness. You know Allah is taking care of things, so you are at peace. Because of that peace, you feel loving and peaceful feelings for others, too.

When you have perfected 1 and 2, you shine!

The Prophet (saw) used to turn his whole body towards someone when they were speaking to him and he used to smile so warmly that it would make everyone around him smile. THAT is shining from inside. Be like that. Shine, and there's nothing you can't do.

 **Your**

Write or doodle to express how you're feeling!